# Mai Ya's Long Journey

## Other Badger Biographies

# Mai Ya's Long Journey

by Sheila Terman Cohen

Wisconsin Historical Society Press

Published by the Wisconsin Historical Society Press
*Publishers since 1855*

**wisconsinhistory.org**

Photographs identified with PH, WHi, or WHS are from the Society's collections; address inquiries about such photos to the Visual Materials Archivist at the above address.

Publications of the Wisconsin Historical Society Press are available at quantity discounts for promotions, fund raising, and educational use. Write to the above address for more information.

Publication of this book was made possible in part by a gift from Highsmith Family Foundation.

Printed in the United States of America

Design by Jill Bremigan

13  12  11  10  09      2  3  4  5  6

Library of Congress Cataloging-in-Publication Data

Cohen, Sheila, 1939–
Mai Ya's long journey / by Sheila Cohen.
    p. cm.—(Badger biographies)
Includes bibliographical references and index.
ISBN 0-87020-365-7 (pbk. : alk. paper)
    Xiong, Mai Ya, 1980—Juvenile literature. 2. Hmong American women—Wisconsin—Madison—Biography—Juvenile literature. 3. Hmong Americans—Wisconsin—Madison—Biography—Juvenile literature. 4. Refugees—Wisconsin—Madison—Biography—Juvenile literature. 5. Refugees—Thailand—Biography—Juvenile literature. 6. Hmong women—Thailand—Biography—Juvenile literature. 7. Madison (Wis.)—Biography—Juvenile literature. I. Title. II. Series.
F589.M19H55 200
305.48'96914'092—dc2
                                        2004028570

∞ The paper used in this publication meets the minimum requirements of the American National Standard for Information Sciences—Permanence of Paper for Printed Library Materials, ANSI Z39.48-1992.

Thanks, as always, to the Highsmith Family
Foundation for its generous gift and
continuing support of our publications.

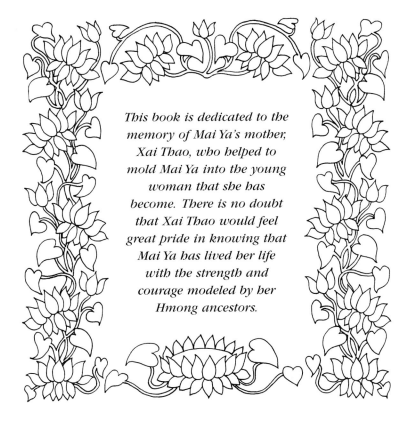

*This book is dedicated to the memory of Mai Ya's mother, Xai Thao, who helped to mold Mai Ya into the young woman that she has become. There is no doubt that Xai Thao would feel great pride in knowing that Mai Ya has lived her life with the strength and courage modeled by her Hmong ancestors.*

# Southeast Asia

Map by Amelia Janes,
Midwest Educational Graphics

# Contents

This story cloth or paj ntaub depicts the Hmong journey from Laos and Thailand to Madison, Wisconsin.

Many Hmong (mong) people believe that the word Hmong means "free people" or "free." Throughout their history, the Hmong people have struggled to be free—often risking their lives in the process. Yet they survive. In many ways, the survival of the Hmong people has come from a feeling of connection as one family. Hmong stories, carried from one generation to the next, teach that all Hmong people are born of one mother. It is in that spirit that generations of Hmong have helped and supported one another, each like a separate thread sewn into a strong fabric.

# Meet Mai Ya

*‍‍‍* ❖ *‍*

*Mai Ya Xiong* (my yah shong) is *Hmong*. She was born
in 1980 in Thailand. She lived with her parents and two
brothers and two sisters in a crowded space within a **refugee**
(**ref y**oo jee) **camp** called *Ban Vinai* (ban vin eye). The camp
was surrounded by a barbed wire fence. It was the only
home Mai Ya had ever known. Then one day, when she was
seven years old, she boarded a bus with her family to pass
through the camp
gate for the first
time in her life.
Although she had
never been on an
airplane before,

These documents
helped the Xiongs travel
to the United States.

Photo by Marcus Cohen

**refugee camp:** A safe place for people forced by war or disaster to leave their homes

Kajsiab House, Photo by Sarah Clement

**Thatched** roof of a traditional Hmong house, built in Madison, Wisconsin

now she was flying halfway around the world. What a long time to be in the air! And when she stepped off the plane, she entered a new country and a new life.

Wisconsin must have seemed like a very strange place to Mai Ya. In Ban Vinai, most of the people around her were Hmong, just like her family. In Wisconsin, people looked very different from her, and they spoke English, not Hmong. This new place was going to take a long time to feel like home! But Mai Ya's long journey really began many years before she stepped onto the bus that took her from Ban Vinai. The Xiong family story began in *Laos* (**lah** os), the country in Southeast Asia where Mai Ya's parents were born.

thatched: Roofing material consisting of plant stalks or leaves, such as reeds or palm fronds

xii

# 1

## Mai Ya's Parents Grow Up in Troubled Laos

When Mai Ya's mother, *Xai Thao* (sy tao), was a young girl, the rooster was her only alarm clock. It crowed every morning at 3:00 a.m. to tell her that it was time to get up and prepare the meals for her family to take to the fields. She would light the fire in the deep pit that occupied the middle of the central room in the house. Then she would go outside to collect water from a nearby stream. Soon others in the family would get up from their bamboo and grass beds that were stretched out on the mud floor along one wall. All began their own early morning tasks.

In the mountain villages of Laos, men built their own homes out of bamboo, wood, and thick grasses called thatch. They fit each part carefully together without using nails. Girls like Xai Thao and boys who were old enough to help their parents worked in the fields tending to crops of corn, rice, and sugar cane. Often they worked from early morning until the sun began to sink low in the sky. Others tended to the chickens, pigs, and cattle that were raised on their land.

Kajsiab House.
Photo by Sarah Clement

This traditional tool is used to pound rice.

As a boy, Mai Ya's father, *Kou Xiong* (koo shong), also awoke early every morning. Hmong villages had no electricity, so he needed to cut wood for the fire that would cook his family's food. Like the daily chores in Xai Thao's house, each person in Kou Xiong's house had a job to do to help the day get started.

When chores were done, a favorite pastime was listening to elders tell tales about the history of their ancestors. Women would sew beautiful designs into cloth called *paj ntaub* (pah dow) meaning flower cloth. And children would make up games played with rocks collected on the ground. Another favorite game was *tub lub* (too loo), a game of spinning tops. Children wind string around a stick and an attached wooden top. Then they throw the tops to the ground so that they spin very fast. The top that goes the farthest wins.

WHS Museum 1996.118.4

The triangle and other shapes and bright colors of a traditional paj ntaub each have a meaning to Hmong.

The Hmong people took great pride in being able to provide for themselves. They farmed their own food, spoke their own language, and practiced the traditions of their culture. They needed little contact with the rest of the world.

When Kou Xiong was about 16, the quiet routine of his home was harshly interrupted. War had broken out in nearby Vietnam, a country directly to the east of Laos. The **Communists (kom** yuh nists) of North Vietnam and the anti-Communists of South Vietnam were fighting. War fanned across the border into the Hmong villages of Laos where Kou's family lived.

**Communists:** Communists believe in communism. Communism is a way of organizing a country where the government owns all the land and factories, and all the people share equally.

At the same time, Kou Xiong knew that trouble was building between a Communist group in Laos called the *Pathet Lao* (pa tet low) and the Lao government that was set in place when the **French colonists** left Laos. Some of the people of Laos believed that a Communist government would improve their lives, so they joined with the Pathet Lao fighters. Many others were afraid that the Communists would rob them of their land and freedom, so they sided with the Lao government. A **civil war** broke out between the clashing sides.

When the United States entered the war in Vietnam, Hmong men and boys fought with the Americans against the Communists. The United States hoped to prevent the Communists from taking control of South Vietnam and Laos. In the United States, that war became known as the Vietnam War.

**French colonists:** The government of France owned and controlled Laos from 1893 until 1954. Laos was a French colony during that time. **Civil war:** A war between groups or regions of the same country

4

# The United States in Vietnam

In the 1960s, the United States entered the war in Vietnam. Before long, the U. S. **Central Intelligence Agency** (CIA) began to secretly **recruit** Kou Xiong and other young Hmong men to fight with in the war against the Communists. But recruiting Hmong men in Laos was against an international agreement called the **Geneva Accords.** The Geneva Accords promised that other nations would leave the independent country of Laos alone.

The American public was not told that the Hmong were fighting to help the U. S. military. The U. S. government decided to keep the Hmong army in Laos a secret, so the Hmong soldiers became known as the secret army. Some of the soldiers were very skilled fighters.

**Central Intelligence Agency:** An agency within the U.S. government that gathers information about other countries for the purpose of keeping the United States secure    **recruit:** To encourage people to join the military service or any organization    **Geneva Accords:** Agreements stating that other countries were not to interfere in Laos

"Many who fought were little boys, no older than 11 or 12," Mai Ya's father remembered many years later. He held his hand at waist level to demonstrate their height. "Many were so small that their machine guns hung down to their ankles when they were strapped on to their shoulders."

One day, young Kou Xiong saw a terrible thing happen. While tending the rows of sugar cane in the fields, he suddenly heard a large explosion. Enemy soldiers from across the border in North Vietnam had entered the village. They threw a bomb that sent flames flying into the air. He saw that the bomb hit the home he shared with his aunt and uncle. He knew that his aunt and uncle were inside.

"When my family was killed, I had to fight back," Kou Xiong said with sadness in his voice. Like so many other young men in his village, he joined the U.S. military. "I did not have much training to be a soldier," Mai Ya's father recalled. "They gave me a parachute and orders to jump from a helicopter into the jungle. American soldiers hid there. We rescued them or brought maps and other supplies. It was very dangerous. You never knew when the enemy was hiding there, too."

In 1975, the American military left Vietnam and Laos. The U. S. government knew that the war in Southeast Asia had been lost to the Communist forces. But the Hmong people of Laos continued to fight and struggle. They hoped that peace would be restored to their villages, and they would once again be free. Unfortunately, the Communist forces greatly outnumbered Hmong troops. Of the almost 400,000 people who lived in the Hmong villages of Laos in 1973, it is believed that about 100,000 lost their lives in the war. By 1975, the Pathet Lao government was in complete power.

The Pathet Lao punished men like Kou Xiong who had fought with the Americans against the Communists during the war. Some were killed. Others were forced to work until they were almost dead. Most of the Hmong people were like prisoners in their own country, robbed of their farmland and dying of starvation.

By the time the Americans left Laos, Xai Thao and Kou Xiong were married. But they were never able to start a real home. Like many other Hmong families, they needed to hide in the heavily forested jungles that surrounded their hillside village.

Xai Thao later remembered what a difficult time it was. "We were so scared. For three years, we had to keep hiding," Mai Ya's mother said, lowering her voice. "We would build a shelter of leaves and sticks in the jungle. We would stay there until it was safe to move on. We would move every three or four days."

At the time, many small children were dying from lack of food and new diseases brought to the villages by people from other places. The Xiongs had a boy and a girl baby, but both died. Fighting back tears years later, Xai Thao said, "They are not with us anymore."

The Xiongs knew that life in Laos was getting too dangerous for them to stay. Like many others, they decided to try to escape Laos. In order to cross to the neighboring

8

country of Thailand, just to the west, they had to cross the Mekong River. They knew they were risking their lives, but felt they had no other choice.

Mai Ya's family was lucky. They survived.

For days, the Xiongs and several other family members crept through the jungle. They quietly and slowly made their way toward the Mekong River, the winding boundary of water between Laos and Thailand. "We ate grasses, weeds, and whatever we could find to stay alive," Mai Ya's father explained, turning his mouth down and squinting his eyes at the thought of it. Finally, after 16 days, they arrived at the bank of the Mekong River.

Photo by Treva Breuch

The Xiongs had to travel through the thick jungles of Laos to get to Thailand.

Photo by ThajYing and Choua Lee

Mekong River

Once on the shore in the dark of the night, they gathered up the hollow bamboo plants that were growing around them. "We could not swim," Kou Xiong continued. "We put bamboo rods under our arms and across our chest to help us float," he said, raising his arms to show how they devised a makeshift life preserver. "The river was very high," he said. "We were afraid."

"Soldiers with guns stood on the shore looking for people who were trying to escape," Xai Thao added. Many people tried to cross the river with babies on their backs. If the baby cried out, it was a signal to the soldiers that someone was there. Sometimes whole families were shot and killed. Others were carried away by the strong river currents and drowned.

"We did not make a sound," Mai Ya's mother recalled. Instead, the Xiongs would signal a message to one another by tightly squeezing each other's hand as they waded and floated through the water.

Photo by Marcus Cohen

This paj ntaub depicts how difficult it was to cross the Mekong River.

# 2

## The Xiong Family's Life in Thailand

Courtesy of the Xiong family

When Mai Ya's parents finally arrived in Thailand, they still did not feel safe. Thai bandits met them on the shore and demanded that they hand over any valuable **silver bar** that they might have with them. "We took only the clothes on our backs," Mai Ya's father explained. "After searching us, they let us go."

The Xiongs finally made it to the Ban Vinai Refugee Camp. Xai Thao remembered their arrival. "So many were crowded into a small space. At first, we were put in a building with other families. Only a bamboo and grass curtain separated one family from another."

Mai Ya as a child at the Ban Vinai Refugee Camp in Thailand

**silver bar:** Bars of silver that were once used for trade (like money) by the Hmong in Laos

In Laos, it was customary to build a home with a view of a nearby mountain from the front door. But in Ban Vinai, that was impossible. Row upon row of thatched grass roofs and wooden walls of hastily built huts became the only view. These buildings were squeezed close together to house the refugees that were arriving every day. When Mai Ya was born, more than 45,000 people were crowded into the camp.

Mai Ya and Xai Thao (both on the right) at the Ban Vinai Refugee Camp

Many of the people who managed to escape Laos arrived at the camp sick or injured. In the early days, the camp did not have enough medicines or doctors. Even food and water were in short supply. "There was no place to go," Kou Xiong said. He also remembered the barbed wire fence that encircled Ban Vinai. "The hardest part was having nothing to do," he sadly remarked, since there were very few jobs for the men in the camp.

Women began sewing a new type of paj ntaub embroidery called story cloths. With delicate stitches on bright blue cloth, they created pictures that told of their lives in Laos and of the difficult escape across the Mekong River. Mai Ya's grandmother and other women sent their needlework to the United States. Relatives who were already living here could sell the story cloths to make a little money.

Mai Ya, her brothers Cher and Lou See, and her sisters Mai Lee and Mai Yee were all born at Ban Vinai. Only her youngest brother, Andrew, was born in the United States. Mai Ya was the only one old enough to attend the school that the United Nations and other organizations set up at the camp.

Wrinkling her nose, as if she had just eaten a sour lemon, Mai Ya described the school at Ban Vinai as "very different from the schools in America. I had to hold up my hands every day to have my fingernails checked. If they were dirty, I might have to lean over and get a paddling or another kind of punishment. One day I had to kneel down with my hands outstretched in front of me. Then the teacher placed heavy rocks on my palms."

Mai Ya in her Ban Vinai school uniform and hat

After living in Ban Vinai for a year, Mai Ya's family was beginning to lose hope of ever leaving. It was still very dangerous to return to Laos as they had planned. The U.S. government allowed a few Hmong military leaders and their families to come to the United States in 1975. But a larger group of Hmong people began coming after 1980. Some people were allowed into other countries, such as Australia and France.

Mai Ya's family did not know what to do. How could they leave without their parents and relatives who would have to stay behind? Rather than leaving Ban Vinai with the first large wave of refugees, they waited for seven more years until Xai Thao's mother was allowed to accompany them to the United States.

Each Hmong family had to have a **sponsor** already living in the United States. Mai Ya had an uncle who had already left Thailand. He was living in the distant city of Madison, Wisconsin. He agreed to be the sponsor for Mai Ya's family.

Courtesy of the Xiong family

Mai Ya's cousins

"Before we left, officials at the camp asked me many questions," Mai Ya's father recalled. They asked, "What was the name of your leader in the war?" and "What was the name of this weapon?" Camp officials wanted to make sure that Kou Xiong had fought with the Americans. "We had to fill out many papers. They helped us with that at the camp."

In 1987, Mai Ya and her family were ready to leave Ban Vinai when Mai Ya was seven years old. Mai Ya's mother described that difficult decision. "It was very hard to say goodbye to friends and family. We did not know if we would ever see them again."

**sponsor:** A person, people, or organization that agrees to help refugees enter the country

16

A well-known Hmong saying helped Xai Thao express one of the strongest Hmong values: "To be with family is to be happy; to be without family is to be lost."

Mai Ya and her family filed onto the large bus that was about to carry them out of the Ban Vinai refugee camp. Some of the people on the bus were reaching out of the windows to touch the hands

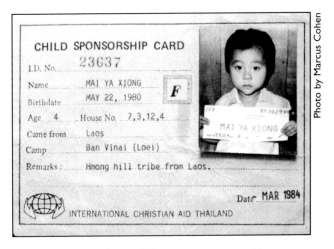

CHILD SPONSORSHIP CARD

I.D. No. 23637

Name          MAI YA XIONG          F

Birthdate     MAY 22, 1980

Age    4      House No.    7,3,12,4

Came from     Laos

Camp          Ban Vinai (Loei)

Remarks :     Hmong hill tribe from Laos.

Date  MAR 1984

INTERNATIONAL CHRISTIAN AID THAILAND

Photo by Marcus Cohen

This document showed that someone would sponsor Mai Ya when she arrived in the United States.

of those who would not be coming with them. Others were waving goodbye with tears in their eyes. The bus began to move. For the first time in their lives, Mai Ya and her sisters and brothers crossed over the boundary of the Ban Vinai refugee camp and entered the world that lay beyond.

# 3

## Mai Ya and Her Family Come to Wisconsin

———————— 🐾 ————————

Except for Kou Xiong, who had flown in a small helicopter, Mai Ya and her family had never been in an airplane before. So, the large plane that lifted them out of Thailand felt like a magic carpet, carrying them to another world and another time.

Courtesy of the Xiong family

Before the war in Laos, Mai Ya's parents could not have possibly imagined that they would one day be living in an apartment in an unheard of place called Madison, Wisconsin. Before coming to the United States, they could not have imagined a stove, a refrigerator,

The Xiong family soon after arriving in the United States

and running water right in their house. In their village, the family used a small pit in the ground as a toilet.

When Mai Ya arrived in Madison in 1987, she and her parents, two sisters, and two brothers shared her uncle's apartment with his family of seven. Her youngest brother, Andrew, was not yet born. Although this apartment would be considered very crowded for 14 people by American standards, it was nothing like the Ban Vinai refugee camp in Thailand. After living in a small wooden hut, the space in the family apartment was much easier to handle.

Mai Ya did not know any English when she arrived in Madison. "It was so strange to hear people talking, but not be able to understand what they were saying," she later remembered. "It was like having the radio on and hearing nothing but static. Everything around me seemed very different."

Because Laos and Thailand are both tropical climates, the temperature there always felt like summer. The Xiongs had arrived in winter. The difference in weather was one thing that Mai Ya recalled sharply. "I had never seen snow before, or felt cold weather. That was a huge surprise." She and her sisters and brothers had the responsibility of shoveling the snow. Once Andrew came along, he loved to play in it. But, of course, he was born in Wisconsin!

Mai Ya's sister, Mai Lee, shovels while her brothers play in the snow.

Madison in winter

Mai Ya's brother, Lou See, in a snowbank

20

Xai Thao remembered, "I was afraid to go out of the house. Maybe I can't find my way home. One day I wait for a bus on the wrong side of the street. I went downtown, but I didn't want to go there." The grocery store was confusing, too. It was nothing like the small outdoor market in the village where everyone would go to sell their chickens, vegetables, or crafts. It was hard to tell what was inside of all the metal cans that lined the shelves. And it was even harder to understand how much money to give to the cashier.

Staring off into the distance as if remembering a bad dream, she said, "Sometimes I wanted to give up."

Thai Ying and Choua Lee

Busy market street in Laos

21

# 4

# Mai Ya Grows Up in Two Worlds

In 1993, just six years after leaving Ban Vinai refugee camp, the Xiongs looked back and found it hard to believe how much their lives had changed. The family had moved into a red brick duplex apartment of their own that felt very large compared to sharing bedrooms, a bathroom, and a kitchen with another family.

The Xiongs in their livingroom

Mai Ya in middle school

Mai Ya in her traditional
Hmong New Year's
holiday clothing

As a seventh grade student at Van Hise Middle School in Madison, Mai Ya's favorite days were the ones when she could eat pizza or subs for lunch in the cafeteria! But the meals that she helped her mother prepare at home each night were still very different from the food that was served at school. One of Mai Ya's favorite dishes at home was shredded papaya in fish sauce. As she helped

Mai Ya helping prepare dinner for her family

23

her mother grate the papaya in a wooden bowl, Andrew and Lou See enjoyed a snack of sticky rice on the floor near their feet.

Lou See and Andrew eating

When Mai Ya entered public school in second grade, she started to attend an English as a Second Language (ESL) class to help her understand and learn to speak English. By the time she reached seventh grade, she was able to speak comfortably with everyone at her school. Mai Ya's English was so good by then that she was appointed to her school's student council. She needed to attend meetings and report information back to her homeroom.

At home, Mai Ya was expected to speak only Hmong with her parents. "That was one of the hardest parts for me," Mai Ya said. "Sometimes I would get all mixed up, and English words would pop into Hmong sentences."

24

Mai Ya's parents went to the local community college with other adults from all over the world to try to learn English, too. "Without English, we cannot go to the

Mai Ya in her ESL class

grocery store, read signs, or get a good job," Kou Xiong said.

Xai Thao shook her head and laughed. "English is very different from Hmong," she said. "In Hmong there are no 's' or 'd' endings on words, so an English word like 'kids' may come out of my mouth sounding like 'kid.' The word 'walked' may sound like 'walk.' "

"One Hmong word may have many meanings," Mai Ya's father explained. "The word *nhia* (nee a) may mean 'sweetheart,' 'now,' or 'mother,' depending on the tone of

Mai Ya talking with friends at her school cafeteria when she was in seventh grade

25

a person's voice. Those who do not grow up speaking a tonal language like Hmong have a difficult time hearing the differences."

Mai Ya's parents did not want their children to forget the Hmong language. "We want our children to have a good education. We want them to have a good life in this country. But, we hope that they will not forget the Hmong ways," said Kou Xiong. As the oldest girl in a Hmong family, Mai Ya was expected to come home

Mai Ya helping Andrew with his snowsuit

from school each day to help her mother cook and take care of her younger sisters and brothers.

"The hardest part of being a Hmong American is trying to follow the rules of both cultures," Mai Ya confided. "Sometimes the Hmong and American customs are very different from one another. Then it is confusing. Then, I'm not sure who I am."

"It is important that our children understand the **rituals** (**rich** oo uhlz) of the elders," her father reminded her. From birth to death, there are rituals to please the good spirits.

The Hmong New Year is the most joyful Hmong celebration. In Laos, it was the time to celebrate the blessings of the rice harvest, to honor one's ancestors, and to give thanks to the good spirits. It was also a time to find a marriage partner.

Women worked all year long to prepare new and beautiful clothing to wear for the festivities. It was believed that anyone who wore old clothing to a New Year celebration might expect bad luck in the coming year.

The New Year celebration in Laos started in December, when the new moon was about to appear in the sky. It could last for many days. Bright flowers grew on the hillsides, as if to match the festive clothing.

**rituals:** A set of actions always performed the same way, often as part of a religion

# An Animist Faith

Many of the Hmong rituals come from **animist** beliefs. Hmong tradition teaches that spirits exist in all of nature—from each blade of grass to every human being. Some of the spirits are believed to be good. Others are not. For example, in Laos, as soon as a child was born, the **placenta** (plah sen tah), the organ that feeds the baby developing within the mother's womb, was buried in a place of honor in the home.

At death, the funeral is one of the most sacred rituals. It is a time to return a person's soul back to its placenta. Funerals usually last for several days or more as the community gathers to listen to the *txiv xai* (ze si) recite a special chant. The room fills with the beat of a large drum and the mournful call of the *rab qeej* (keng), used to accompany the soul on its journey. It is a way of releasing the soul from its earthly world so that it can again be born as a new baby.

**animist:** Belief that spirits exist in all of nature

28

Originally the New Year's celebration in Wisconsin was switched from December to the fall season so the festivities could take place outside, as they had in Laos. Hmong families met in a large park. Everyone from the youngest babies, in hand-stitched baby carriers called *dlaim hlab-nyas,* (dlee hala nee a) to the most respected clan elders, gathered to greet each other.

Photo by Marcus Cohen

Rab qeej player

Each year out in an open soccer field in the park, young men and boys from different **clans** played a soccer match to see which clan will become the champions for the year. Soccer became a favorite game when it was played to pass the long hours in the refugee camps.

**clans:** The Hmong are divided into at least 18 major clans, each with their own leaders. Clan members bear the name of their clan throughout life.

A small group of teenage girls usually played volleyball, a new custom that started in the United States. "Many Hmong people still think that girls are not supposed to wear shorts and play such games," Mai Ya remarked.

In 1993, Mai Ya and her younger sister, Mai Lee, appeared in their traditional dresses with brightly colored **batik** (bah **teek**) sashes and dark turbans wound upon their heads. Silver coins dangled from their hats, purses, and wide sashes, making cheerful musical sounds as they walked. Mai Ya and Mai Lee, like many others, wore silver necklaces that hung nearly to their waists. Their looped chains and ornaments glittered in the sun.

Young women in traditional clothes

**batik:** A method of dyeing a fabric by which the parts of the fabric not intended to be dyed are covered with removable wax

30

Mai Ya and Mai Lee joined a long line that was forming. They stood side by side with other young women and girls in traditional clothing. Some of the women carried parasols. Different types of dress represented different groups of Hmong who came from different areas of Laos. Young men, dressed in traditional hats and jackets and loose-fitting black pants, lined up opposite them. They were about to play the *pov pob* (**pow** pow) game.

"It took many hours to prepare my daughters' clothes for the New Year," Mai Ya's mother said, as she stood by the sidelines watching her daughters with pride. Xai Thao did

Hmong New Year in Madison

not play pov pob, since it is only played by children or young women who are not married. In Laos, it was not unusual for a young woman to marry at the age of 14 or 15.

Soon the women began to chant poetry in a haunting rhythm. At the same time, they tossed a small ball made of soft black cloth back and forth to the boys facing them. "Whenever someone drops the ball, they are supposed to give away something special, like a silver coin or piece of jewelry, to the person who threw it," Xai Thao explained. Returning the item gave the boy and girl a chance to see each other again.

For a minute, onlookers at the park in Madison might have thought that they were in a Laotian mountain village, with the boys and girls in their traditional clothes, and the sounds of chanting and singing.

But, as a reminder of the changes that had taken place by 1993, another girl ran to join the line of pov pob players. Her traditional dress was replaced by black shorts and a

Photo by Marcus Cohen

Pov pob line

Photo by Marcus Cohen

Playing pov pob

loosely fitting gray sweatshirt. Kneeling down like a baseball catcher, she threw a green tennis ball to a boy opposite her.

"Today, pov pob is usually played just for fun," Xai Thao explained. "But in Laos, it was played to choose someone to marry." When a man saw a

33

# Silver Necklaces

It is believed that silver necklaces were first worn to remind people of the time in China when the Hmong people were used as slaves and were forced to wear large locks around their

necks. Later, owning silver was thought to be a sign of having worked hard, since silver was used in trade for goods produced. Those wearing it long ago would gain the respect of others. In more recent times, an aluminum necklace may replace a silver one that was left behind during the escape from Laos. But girls still wear these necklaces as a reminder of the past.

Photo by Alan Ginsberg

Traditional Hmong silver necklace

woman he liked, he threw the ball to her to express his feelings. Later they would talk. He would visit her home and would "speak" of love by playing a small musical instrument called a *ncas*, or jaw harp. In Laos, boys and girls were not allowed to show affection for one another in public by holding hands or hugging.

Girls with parasols

When the boy and girl decided to marry, he would go to the girl's home and take her away to live with his family. The boy's family was expected to pay a certain amount to the girl's family as a sign of respect. This amount was called a bride price and was usually paid in silver bar.

Mai Ya throwing the pov pob ball

35

Photo by Treva Breuch

Young man playing the jaw harp

Although many Hmong rituals of courtship have changed in this country, some have not.

The Hmong people are made up of least 18 clans, or separate groups, each with its own last name and leader. People in the same clan think of each other as Americans think of a member of their family. For example, the word for "sister," *tus mua* (too moo ah), or for "brother," *tus nus* (too noo), is often used when speaking of a person in the same clan. To show respect, young people call an elder "aunt," "uncle," "mother," "father," "grandmother," or "grandfather." Even at 12 years old, Mai Ya knew that when she was ready to marry, she could not marry anyone sharing her father's clan name. "It would be like marrying a brother," she said.

As the pov pob game was about to end, everyone could smell the spices and flavors of familiar food. In the corner of the park, egg rolls, chicken, rice, and vegetable

Photo by Marcus Cohen

greens covered long picnic tables, inviting everyone to come and enjoy.

In the evening, Mai Ya and her family attended New Year activities held at a nearby high school. When familiar music of Laos and Thailand filled the large gym, Mai Ya and Mai Lee ran with several other young girls to change into their dance outfits. They were going to perform the traditional dances that they had learned from a Hmong woman at the community center.

Learning such dances is another way to keep the past alive. "Our hands and feet move in different ways," Mai Ya said. She demonstrated with a graceful twist of the wrist.

37

Photo by Bob Rashid

Each dance tells a story of harvesting rice, picking flowers, or growing up in a mountain village.

After the last group of dancers left the floor, the music suddenly switched to a loud, fast beat. Several teenage girls and boys ran out on the high school stage wearing jeans and white shirts. They began to do a rock dance. That year, a brand new sound was added to the celebration. The large, brightly colored words behind the dancers read *Nyob Zoo Xyoo Tshiab* (na zhong shong **chi** a). Beneath those words, **HAPPY NEW YEAR** was spelled out in equally bold letters.

Those like Mai Ya who were growing up as Hmong Americans again found themselves living in two worlds.

Photo by Marcus Cohen

Girl dancing at Hmong New Year celebration

# 5

## Hmong Traditional Beliefs

Some Hmong families have become Christian since their arrival in the United States. Yet, most Hmong people feel that it is important to carry on many of the traditions of their animist faith. At special times, a **shaman** (shah mun) comes to the family home to ask that good spirits enter and that bad spirits keep away.

In Laos, days before the New Year celebration, each family worked hard to clean the house and prepare foods to please the house spirit, *xwm kab* (sou kah). The family also performed rituals to honor their ancestors and prayed to the good spirits to bring health and good fortune in the coming year.

In Wisconsin, many people gathered early in the morning at Mai Ya's house to honor the traditions of their homeland.

---

**shaman:** A person believed to have close contact with the spirit world and therefore trusted as a healer

Members of the Xiong and Thao clans came from near and far to take part in the event.

Every room in Mai Ya's house hummed with activity. Mai Ya's aunts and other women from the clan sat at a table in the kitchen. They placed shredded vegetables on rectangles of thin rice dough. Then the women rolled the dough to make *kab yob* (kah yo), or what Americans call egg rolls.

Mai Ya's mother stood at the stove mixing the contents of a large steaming pot. Turning from the pot, Xai Thao explained, "This is *fawm* (fur), a favorite soup." She stirred the spicy broth, allowing noodles and vegetables to rise to the top. Mai Ya's youngest sister, Mai Yee, added that the soup is made with lemongrass. As she watched her mother, she widened her eyes and licked her lips, thinking of the feast to come.

Downstairs in the basement there was more activity. Kou Xiong and other men chopped meat on large wooden blocks. They were getting ready to prepare *laj* (lah), a favorite meat dish that is made with hot pepper over rice.

As the younger children played outside on the lawn, the shaman stood at the open door of the kitchen, chanting quietly. He tossed two buffalo horns onto the ground once, twice, and then again. Mai Ya explained that the horns must fall in the right direction in order to call the ancestors' spirits to a home.

A vase of red flowers stood on the long table in the front room. The color red is thought to get rid of any bad spirits. There was a large bowl containing rice, many cooked eggs, and two long sticks of burning incense. The family placed these things on the table to please the souls of family ancestors, inviting them to bless the New Year and bring good luck.

Before eating, the shaman closely examined the cooked chicken on the table before him. It is believed that if the chicken's claw is not pointed in the right direction, the good spirits will not visit the house. Everyone smiled and laughed when the shaman reported that the chicken was a good one. The shaman prayed, and the eating began.

After the meal, the *khi tes* (**key** tay) ceremony begins. The khi tes ceremony calls the ancestors' spirits to bring blessings to the family. As part of the ceremony, ties are

Photo by Marcus Cohen

Shaman at the table

placed around the wrist to keep good spirits within the body.

In the corner of the room, Mai Ya began to wind white yarn from her elbow to the crook of her thumb. She and some of her friends measured and cut the yarn into many smaller pieces. "The shaman and other clan members tie the white strands around the wrists of each person in the house," Mai Ya said, as she collected the white strands and placed them in a pile. "They are tied on the wrists to help the good spirits stay within the body. It's the Hmong way of wishing everyone good health and good fortune in the coming year."

Today, the New Year celebration has again been changed to fit new times. Instead of celebrating the holiday in the fall of

Note the white ties on Mai Ya's wrist from the khi tes ceremony.

the year, the Hmong elders have chosen to return the celebration to the traditional month of December. "In Wisconsin, the New Year is very different than it was in Laos," Mai Ya comments. "It's too cold outside in the winter so everyone piles into a large hall at the county Convention Center." Though the old traditions of pov pob and Hmong food remain, a few American touches have been added. There is now a Miss Hmong America contest and a fashion show that features the traditional dress of each clan. Neon ceiling lights have replaced the sun shining on the lush green mountainsides.

A long time ago, when Hmong people lived in China, they were forbidden to write in their own

Children dancing at Hmong New Year celebration

43

language because the Chinese
rulers believed that they would
not accept or change to Chinese
ways. It was not until the early
1950s that the Hmong language
was written down by Christian
missionaries. Until that time,

Mai Ya reading to Andrew

Photo by Bob Rashid

information was communicated by word-of-mouth, and beliefs
were passed on through folktales told by elders to the children
of the next generation.

One of Mai Ya's favorite folktales that her grandmother told
her as she was growing up is on the next page. Mai Ya, in turn,
has shared it with her younger sisters and brothers. She may
someday pass it on to her own children.

To Mai Ya, her family, and the many other Hmong families
who have traveled from quiet mountain villages to the fast-
paced world of computers and jet planes, the New Year
celebration, the khi tes ceremony, the funeral traditions, and the
folktales are necessary links to their past. They are important
reminders that the rich Hmong culture, though changing, must
not be forgotten.

# The Beginning of Night and Day

Very long ago, there were nine suns and nine moons. Day and night lasted such a long time that the people could not work enough to grow food. They were angry and made a crossbow to shoot the suns and the moons. The suns and the moons were very frightened of the people, and so they would not come out at all. Then there was darkness. The people could not make the darkness go away, so they sent a bull to call the suns and moons out of hiding. They did not come. Then they sent a tiger, but still, there was darkness. Next they sent a bird, but the suns and moons would not come out. At last, they sent a rooster. The rooster called and called. Finally, the suns came out for a little while and then the moons came out for a little while. And that was the beginning of night and day. From then on, the people were able to work and grow enough food for everyone.

# 6

# Mai Ya Continues Her Journey in Two Worlds

———————— 🐾 ————————

It has been a long journey for Mai Ya from the huts of Ban Vinai refugee camp to the college classrooms of the University of Wisconsin-Milwaukee where she completed her studies and graduated in December 2004. It has not been an easy journey, but it has been a remarkable one.

At her college graduation ceremony, Mai Ya gives her young niece a hug.

🐾 🐾 🐾

Shortly after Mai Ya's seventh grade year, she and her family faced another tragedy that not even war had prepared them for. On June 11, 1993, Mai Ya's mother, her grandmother, and her aunt were killed in a car accident. "Losing my mother was a great loss for me. Not only did I

The Xiongs at Xai Thao's grave site

lose my mother, but I lost a great friend as well," Mai Ya recalled. "I cried so hard that my body felt numb. Finally, I couldn't cry anymore." True to the Hmong culture, Mai Ya said, "Our family and clan were there for us when we needed them. Many clan members surrounded our family with food, caring, and prayers for days after the accident." One of Mai Ya's aunts and uncles moved from La Crosse, Wisconsin, to Madison to help Kou Xiong as Mai Ya and her sisters and brothers were growing up.

47

Even with help from family and clan members, it was necessary for Mai Ya to become the main cook and caretaker for her younger sisters and brothers when her father was at work. "It was a very hard time for me," she said. "Sometimes I just wanted to be with my friends at school when I knew I had to go home and help."

Now that she's grown up, Mai Ya looks back at that period of her life and says, "I really feel that the struggles I faced along the way have helped to make me the strong person I am today." Mai Ya has shown her strength in many ways over the years. In spite of the tragedy and the pulls on her time at home, she managed by keeping herself involved with the Hmong community and in activities at East High School in Madison. Many of her activities centered around trying to understand her culture and her role in it. As a Hmong American, she was beginning to think about where she fit into both her Hmong and American worlds.

Mai Ya needed to sort things out. So she and three of her friends organized a group called Hmong American Youth Organization. Once a week, Hmong boys and girls would get together to discuss the confusion that they felt about being wedged between two very different worlds. How could they live up to their parents' Hmong expectations and still fit into their American lives at school?

Sometimes they invited their parents to meet with them. They talked about their problems. "If I wear baggy pants, it doesn't mean that I belong to a gang," one of the boys said. "When I have to stay late at school instead of coming right home, why won't you trust me?" one of the girls asked. In turn, their parents told them why they thought it was so important not to lose the Hmong traditions. "Listening and talking with one another felt good," Mai Ya said. "It was a long process, but I think it helped both kids and parents to understand each other a little better."

Looking back, Mai Ya confides, "When I was younger, I worked so hard to be 'American.' I wanted to wear American clothes, eat American food, listen to American music, and celebrate American holidays. Everyone I knew wanted his or her appearance to be 'cool.' Maybe that was because we never saw anything in books, or anywhere else, that represented the Hmong culture. Most American people didn't even know that my father had helped the American soldiers fight in the Vietnam War."

But Mai Ya began to change. "As I got older, I began to understand what my father and mother had been through. Their courage has had a big impact on my life," Mai Ya said. "A big impact," she repeated softly.

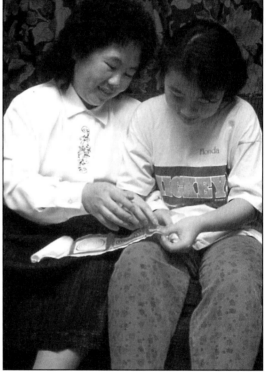

By the time Mai Ya was in high school, she knew she wanted to do something to help young people appreciate and preserve their Hmong heritage. At the same time, she wanted to succeed as a Hmong American. Getting a

Mai Ya's mother, Xai Thao, teaching her paj ntaub

Photo by Treva Breuch

good education became part of her goal. She was happy to receive a **scholarship** (**skah** ler ship) to an after-school program at the University of Wisconsin when she was a freshman at East High School. The program helped young people achieve in school by offering tutoring help. It also provided information about what high school kids needed to do to prepare for college. "It was fun to be on a university campus," Mai Ya said. "It made me wish that someday I could go to a real college."

Courtesy of the Xiong family

Mai Ya's graduation from high school

With a lot of hard work, Mai Ya made her wish come true. Although her family could not afford to send her to college, she was able to get several scholarships to help her go to the University of Wisconsin in Madison when she graduated from East High School.

**scholarship:** Money or aid given to a student to continue studying

51

While there, she continued to be involved with the Hmong community. She was in the Hmong American Student Organization and the Asian American Student Union on campus. These organizations helped Asian students express their needs to the university. One of Mai Ya's proudest moments came in the year 2000 when she was

Photo by Marcus Cohen

Mai Ya's high school graduation party. Notice the ties on Mai Ya's wrist that mean good health and good fortune.

selected Miss Hmong Wisconsin—a new tradition from the American culture that has entered the Hmong New Year celebration.

"It's about more than appearance," Mai Ya explained. "The person selected needs to be in touch with the Hmong culture." As Miss Hmong Wisconsin, Mai Ya committed herself to giving back to the Hmong community. She began a Girl Scout troop for middle school Hmong girls. Most of them had been born in the United States, and knew little about life as it had been in Laos. Mai Ya taught them about

Courtesy of the Xiong family

Mai Ya being crowned Miss Lao-Hmong Wisconsin

some of the Hmong traditions and led discussions about the conflicts they would face as Hmong Americans. "Sometimes it helps to talk about your problems with other people your age," Mai Ya said, remembering her own experiences in high school.

Mai Ya also began to teach girls traditional dances, just as she had learned them at the community center when she was younger. Mai Ya recognized that learning these traditions was a very important part of being a Hmong American. For that reason, she began to teach others at the United Asian

Services of Wisconsin. This local refugee office began in the 1980s to help people with the basic needs of learning English and finding a job. Now, some of those same people are themselves leaders in the community.

With all of Mai Ya's activities and home responsibilities, it became harder and harder for her to keep up with her studies at the university. She made a decision that she must leave Madison to finish her degree at the University of Wisconsin in Milwaukee. "It was the most difficult decision that I've ever made in my life," she said, sitting at the computer in her cramped bedroom near the university campus in Milwaukee. "It meant leaving my family. It meant that I could not be as helpful as a sister and daughter. But I realized that, if I really wanted to help, I needed to make something of myself."

To Mai Ya, making something of herself meant graduating with a double degree in business and marketing. Walking to a class in the business school, Mai Ya said, "I want to be a role model so that other Hmong kids will realize they don't have to limit their opportunities."

Mai Ya at her computer at the University of Wisconsin–Milwaukee

For Mai Ya, her generation of Hmong Americans, and their parents, much has changed in the process of resettlement. The New Year celebration has moved inside. Fluorescent lighting has replaced the outdoor sunshine. Vending booths selling CDs line the walls of a large convention hall. Most of the traditional clothing appears on the stage in a costume show. And beauty pageants have become a large part of the entertainment. Still, there is the playing of the rab qeej as a strong reminder of what had been.

Hmong traditions of courtship and marriage have also begun to change. Though many of the older generation still expect women to marry young and begin a family, Mai Ya admits, "I'm glad that I've resisted that pressure." With a big smile Mai Ya says, "I am the first girl in my family to be graduating from college."

Mai Ya wasn't sure how her father felt about her shift from the Hmong tradition until she heard him talking to one of his friends who questioned why Mai Ya wasn't married at age 14. "She's smart," Kou Xiong answered. "That was the moment I knew that my dad was proud of me," Mai Ya said, wiping away the tears that began to well up in her eyes.

Many Hmong women have replaced their needles and thread with business cards. There is little time to sew paj ntaub, and so it is mainly the elders who carry on that art. Children are sometimes unable to speak to their grandparents because they have lost much of the Hmong language. "My mother taught me the language when I was younger," Mai Ya said. "Now I can't read or write it," she adds with regret. "That's something I want to learn someday."

Mai Ya on campus at UW–Milwaukee

Photo by Marcus Cohen

Out of necessity, traditions, like the New Year celebration, have changed. Many changes reflect the new life that Hmong people have made for themselves in Wisconsin and other states throughout the country. They have made adjustments. And yet, there is something very basically Hmong that remains. For Mai Ya, it is the sense of family connection that is so deeply a part of in the Hmong culture.

"With all we've been through, we are always there for one another," she remarks. "If my parents hadn't taught me the Hmong way of life, I would not be who I am today." Smiling broadly, Mai Ya adds, "I am proud to be Hmong. And what will be lost if we don't preserve some of our traditions? We will eventually lose who we are. That would be a big loss."

# Afterword

In December 2003, the U.S. government ruled to allow a new wave of Hmong refugees to enter the country. In the summer of 2004, the new group began to arrive in the United States. They had been living in poor conditions at a makeshift refugee camp called *Wat Tham Krabok* (wot tom kra bok) in Thailand. The new arrivals had been looking for a home since the official refugee camps closed over ten years ago.

Wat Tham Krabok
Refugee Camp

Photo by John Doman.
Courtesy of the St. Paul Pioneer Press

Eventually, about 15,000 refugees will arrive. Like those who arrived earlier, they will come needing to learn English and to adjust to American ways. As the newest generation of Hmong children become a part of the American culture we hope that, like Mai Ya, these children will learn about and preserve many of the values and traditions that are a part of their rich Hmong heritage.

# Appendix

## *Fighting to be Free*

No one is sure where the Hmong people had their beginnings. Some historians believe that they may have lived in parts of Europe in ancient times and then migrated south to Asia. They have found that Hmong clans did exist in central China 5,000 years ago. But the Hmong were not Chinese and wanted to keep their independence from China. They preserved their own traditions, dress, and language. But the Chinese rulers resented their efforts to remain independent and punished them harshly, even using them as slaves.

In the late 18th century, when the founders of the United States were fighting for independence from English rule, the Hmong continued to fight for their independence in China. Many Hmong people were killed. Though the largest number of Hmong people in the world still live in China today, many decided to leave and migrate southward to Thailand, Vietnam, and Laos in search of freedom. Most of the Hmong people ended up settling in the heavily forested highlands of Laos. The Lao rulers left them alone to live together and practice their own traditions.

In the late 19th century, when French colonists took control of Laos, the Hmong fought to protect their freedom. They fought for their independence again in the 1940s when Japan invaded Laos during World War II. Throughout their history, the Hmong people have risked their lives to keep their independence. Over and over, they managed to stay together and remain a free people.

The Hmong resettlement has become an important part of United States and Wisconsin history. Wisconsin's Hmong population is topped only by California and Minnesota.

# Hmong Time Line

**1500s** – Hmong clans live in south China.

**Late 1700s** – Hmong fight for freedom in China as American colonies fight for independence from England (1776).

**Early 1800s** – Thousands of Hmong migrate from south China to Southeast Asia. Most settle in the highlands of Laos in an area called the Plain of Jars.

**1893** – French occupy Indochina (known today as Laos, Cambodia, Vietnam).

**1940** – Japan invades French Indochina and occupies Laos until end of World War II. Hmong soldiers help French to fight against Japanese invasion.

**Early 1950s** – Hmong language is written by American and French missionaries.

**1954** – French rule ended.

**1954 & 1962** – International agreements called **Geneva Accords** grant independence to Laos and pledge that other countries will not interfere.

**Mid-1950s** – Royal Laotian government (backed by the United States) and Nationalist **Pathet Lao** form two separate groups in Laos.

**1961** – United States enters the Vietnam War to help South Vietnam stop the spread of a **Communist** form of government in North Vietnam.

**1961** – U. S. government and Central Intelligence Agency (CIA) recruit Hmong soldiers in Laos to help in the fight as a secret army against North Vietnam. Hmong General Vang Pao leads the Hmong troops.

**1961** – Pathet Lao sides with Communist North Vietnam.

**1975** – United States military pulls out of Southeast Asia.

**1975** – General Vang Pao and other heads of the army are airlifted out of Laos to the United States. Hmong families are left in danger of enemy troops.

**1975-1992** – One-third of the Hmong population flees Laos. They escape across the Mekong River to hastily built refugee camps in Thailand.

**1980** – U.S. government allows first large wave of Hmong refugees into the country.

**2004** – A new group of Hmong refugees enters the United States after living many years in a makeshift temple in Thailand called Wat Tham Krabok.

# Mai Ya's Time Line

**1967–1975** – Mai Ya's father, Kou Xiong, helps the United States during the Vietnam War.

**1979** – Mai Ya's family escapes Laos for the Ban Vinai Refugee Camp in Thailand.

**1980** – Mai Ya is born at Ban Vinai.

**1987** – Mai Ya and her family leave Ban Vinai for Madison, Wisconsin.

**1993** – Mai Ya and her family record their story. Mai Ya is in the seventh grade at Van Hise Middle School in Madison.

Mai Ya's mother, grandmother, and aunt are killed in a car accident.

**1998** – Mai Ya graduates from Madison East High School.

**2000-2001** – Mai Ya is crowned Miss Lao-Hmong Wisconsin.

**2004** – Mai Ya graduates from UW-Milwaukee with a B.A. degree in Finance and Marketing.

# Glossary

**animist**  One who believes that spirits exist in all of nature

**Ban Vinai** (ban vin eye)*  Refugee camp built in northeastern Thailand to house earliest refugees escaping from Laos

**batik** (bah **teek**)  A method of dyeing a fabric by which the parts of the fabric not intended to be dyed are covered with removable wax

**Central Intelligence Agency** (CIA)  An agency within the U.S. government that gathers information about other countries for the purpose of keeping the United States secure

**civil war**  A war between groups or regions of the same country

**clans**  The Hmong are divided into at least 18 major clans, each with their own leaders.  Every clan member bears the name of their clan throughout life. The most common clan names include: Cha, Fang, Her, Khong, Kue, Lee, Lor, Moua, Pha, Thao, Vang, Vue, Xiong, and Yang. The Hmong are also divided into groups called White, Blue, Green, Black, Striped, and Flowery. Although these groupings mark slight differences in language dialect and clothing, they are of little importance compared to the strong bond that exists among fellow clan members.

**Communists**  Communists believe in communism. Communism is a way of organizing a country where the government owns all the land and factories, and all the people share equally.

**dlaim hlab-nyas** (dlee hala nee a) A baby carrier sewn by the grandmother on the mother's side and presented upon the baby's birth

**fawm** (fur) A spicy soup made with lemongrass, noodles, and vegetables

**French colonists** The government of France owned and controlled Laos from 1893 until 1954. Laos was a French colony during that time.

**Geneva Accords** Two international agreements signed in 1954 and 1962 granting independence to Laos and promising that other countries would not interfere

**heritage** Traditions and culture passed on by ancestors

**kab yob** (kah yo) A soup prepared with noodles, vegetables, and lemongrass

**khi tes** (**key** tay) A ceremony held when there is a birth, wedding, new year, or arrival of a new clan member into the country. Good spirits are called upon to bestow blessings. As part of the ceremony, ties are placed around the wrist to keep good spirits within the body.

**laj** (lah) A dish that is made of chopped meat, hot pepper, and rice

**Mai** (my) A girl's name meaning daughter. Mai is the first part of many girl's names. Other names come from things found in nature, such as Pa Chia, or bright flower.

**ncas** (dja) Jaw harp. Instrument played by young men at time of courtship

**Nyob Zoo Xyoo Tshiab** (na zhong shong **chi** a) The way to say "Happy New Year" in Hmong

**paj ntaub** (pah dow)  Flowery cloth stitchery which appears on clothing, ceremonial items, folktales, and storycloths.  Designs may represent different symbols, such as elephant foot, cucumber seed, or rooster comb.

**Pathet Lao** (pa tet low)  Communist group in Laos

**placenta**  The organ that feeds the baby developing within the mother's womb

**pov pob** (**pow** pow)  A game played with a soft, black cotton ball that was part of a ritual of courtship during the Hmong New Year

**rab qeej** (keng)  Instrument used for ceremonial music that is played at funerals and during the Hmong New Year

**recruit**  To encourage people to join the military service or any organization

**refugee**  Person having to flee his or her country in order to find safety or freedom

**rituals** (**rich** oo uhlz)  A set of actions always performed the same way, often as part of a religion

**scholarship** (**skah** ler ship)  Money or aid given to a student to continue studying

**shaman**  A person believed to have close contact with the spirit world and therefore  trusted as a healer

**silver bar**  Bars of silver that were once used for trade (like money) by the Hmong in Laos

**sponsor**  A person, people, or organization that agrees to help refugees enter the country

**Thao** (tow)  Xai Thao's name differs from her husband's and children's last name because a Hmong woman keeps her father's clan name, even after marriage.

**thatched**  Roofing material consisting of plant stalks or leaves, such as reeds or palm fronds

**txiv neeb** (ze **neng**)  Shaman. A person believed to possess spiritual powers. Used by the clan to call the good spirits and get rid of the bad. The txiv neeb is thought to be a person of special wisdom that serves as a healer and counselor.

**tub lub** (too loo)  A favorite Hmong game played in Laos with a stick and a wooden top

**tus mua** (too moo a)  A sister, which often refers to any girl in the same clan

**tus nus** (too noo)  Sister referring to a brother. In English, there is only one word for "brother" and "sister." In Hmong, there are several different words for family members which help to show the exact relationship. Such words indicate the role a person plays in the family, as well as the degree of respect that must be shown. Elders are always shown the most respect.

**xwm kab** (sou kah)  The protective house spirit, one of the most important spirits

*Hmong words and transliterations vary according to the dialect of the group to which the speaker belongs.

# Reading Group Guide and Activities

## Discussion Questions

❧ What does it feel like to move to a strange place, whether a new classroom, neighborhood, city, or country? Think of all the times that you've been a stranger. Did you feel excited, lonely, afraid, out-of-touch, or stupid? Did you have to learn new things? Have your group brainstorm the feelings that you recall.

❧ Each immigrant, old or young, has unique experiences. How did moving to the United States affect different members of Mai Ya's family? Who had the hardest time? Why? Who had the easiest time? Why?

❧ There were many times when Mai Ya and her parents had to make difficult decisions. What were three of these turning points? What were your reasons for making your selections?

## Activities and Projects

❧ Use the interviewing guidelines in *They Came to Wisconsin Teacher's Guide and Student Materials,* page 94, or create your own interview questions to ask someone who came from another country. If you have a Hmong classmate or know a Hmong elder, interview him or her about experiences before and after arriving in the United States. Which part of the interview meant most to you? Why?

If there is a Hmong student in your class, invite his or her parent or family member to come to the class. Prepare interview questions in advance, based on Mai Ya's experiences. Then compare and contrast with her journey and settlement. Make story cloths that reflect each journey.

Use the turning points idea above to create illustrations for each of the turning points you selected. Mount them on a poster board, and write captions that explain why these events were so important to Mai Ya and her family.

Create your own illustrated time line of Mai Ya's life. The time line in the appendix will help you.

# To Learn More about the Hmong

Chan, Anthony. *Hmong Textile Designs.* Owings Mills, MD: Stemmer House Publishers, Inc., 1990.

Coburn, Jewell Reinhart with Tzexa Cherta Lee. *Jouanah: A Hmong Cinderella.* Arcadia, CA: Shen's Books, 1996.

Edwards, Michelle. *Pa Lia's First Day.* New York: Harcourt, Brace, & Co., 1999.

*A Free People: Our Stories, Our Voices, Our Dreams.* Minneapolis: Hmong Youth Cultural Awareness Project, 1994.

*Future Hmong* at www.futurehmong.com.

Giacchino-Baker, Rosalie (PhD). *The Story of Mah: A Hmong "Romeo and Juliet" Folktale.* El Monte, CA: Pacific Asia Press, 1995.

Goldfarb, Mace. *Fighters, Refugees, and Immigrants: A Story of the Hmong.* Minneapolis: Carolrhoda Books, 1982.

*Laos In Pictures.* Minneapolis: Lerner Publications Company, 1996.

Livo, Norma J. and Dia Cha. *Folk Stories of the Hmong: Peoples of Laos, Thailand, and Vietnam.* Englewood, CO: Libraries Unlimited, Inc., 1991.

Millett, Sandra. *The Hmong of Southeast Asia.* Minneapolis: Lerner Publications, 2002.

Murphy, Nora. *A Hmong Family.* Minneapolis: Lerner Publications Company, 1997.

Pfaff, Tim. *Hmong in America: Journey from a Secret War.* Eau Claire, WI: Chippewa Valley Museum Press, 1995.

Pferdehirt, Julia. *They Came to Wisconsin.* Madison, WI: Wisconsin Historical Society Press, 2003.

Rendon, Marcie R. and Cheryl Walsh Bellville. *Farmer's Market: Families Working Together.* Minneapolis, MN: Carolrhoda Books, 2001.

Roop, Peter and Connie. *The Hmong in America: We Sought Refuge Here.* Appleton, WI: Appleton Area School District, 1990.

Shea, Pegi Deitz. *The Whispering Cloth: A Refugee's Story.* Honesdale, PA: Boyds Mills Press, 1995.

Thao, Cher. *Only a Toad: A Bilingual Hmong Folk Tale.* Adapted by Brian and Heather Marchant. Green Bay, WI: Project Chong, 1993.

Vang, Lue and Judy Lewis. *Grandmother's Path, Grandfather's Way.* Folsom, CA: Folsom-Cordova School System, 1984.

Xiong, Blia. *Nine-in-One: Grr! Grr!: A Folktale from the Hmong People of Laos.* Adapted by Cathy Spagnoli. San Francisco: Children's Book Press, 1989.

Xiong, Ia. *The Gift: The Hmong New Year.* El Monte, CA: Pacific Asia Press, 1996.

# Acknowledgments

This book would not have been possible without hours of interviews with the Xiong family. Mai Ya's parents, Xai Thao and Kou Xiong, relived painful struggles and emotional triumphs as they recounted their story. They did so with generous spirits and welcoming hearts. I am grateful to have had the opportunity to know them.

I appreciate the help I received from Choe Thao, a member of the Hmong community in Madison, Wisconsin, who gave generously of his time and translating skills in order to enhance the mutual understanding and clarity of communication between the author and the Xiong family.

Thank you to Bob Rashid, a nationally recognized Madison photographer, whose photos grace the cover of this book and some of the inside pages. Other photos, taken by Treva Breuch, Marcus Cohen, Alan Ginsberg, ThajYing and Choua Lee of United Refugee Services, and the Xiong family are greatly appreciated. With their talents, all the photographers have helped to provide a visual account of Mai Ya's story. John Robinson of the Madison Children's Museum, Joe Kapler and Andy Kraushaar of the Wisconsin Historical Society, and Mai Ying of Kajsiab House also provided invaluable assistance in obtaining images. Thanks to Shaw Vang for his careful review of information for cultural authenticity and accuracy.

Others at the Wisconsin Historical Society made *Mai Ya's Long Journey* a reality. My editor, Bobbie Malone, established this book as the first in the Badger Biography series; Erica Schock kept this book on track in countless ways; Sarah Clement scanned the images and set up the photo log; Christine Schelshorn and designer Jill Bremigan gave the book its unique feel. Megan Schliesman of the Cooperative Children's Book Center at UW–Madison and Patty Schultz, librarian at Lincoln Elementary School in Madison, pointed out additional resources on the Hmong experience for the bibliography.

And a special thanks to Mai Ya, who has spent many hours sharing her experiences in photos and words. Through her, I have come to understand the hardships and successes that the Hmong people have encountered on their long journey to Wisconsin.

# Author's Note

I began teaching English as a Second Language (ESL) in the Madison schools in 1979, just before the first large group of Hmong children arrived in Wisconsin soon after the end of the Vietnam War. While I was teaching the children in the classroom, I had the opportunity to meet many of their families. I was also invited to clan celebrations and attended funerals within the Hmong community. I was impressed by the warmth and generosity of the Hmong people in the shadow of tremendous hardship and stress. I wanted to know more about them and their journey.

Mai Ya was in the ESL program at Randall Elementary when I first got to know her and her family. In 1993, when she was in the seventh grade at Van Hise Middle School in Madison, Wisconsin, she and her parents shared the story of their long journey with me.

This book is their story. I will always be grateful to them for teaching me so much. Although it is the Xiong family story, it resembles the stories of the almost 200,000 Hmong people who now live in the United States. All of their tales tell of the courage of those who have come here and still struggle to remain a "free people." The Hmong journeys add an important chapter to American history.

Although I have since retired from teaching, as a writer I often explore issues that affect immigrant and refugee populations. I also served on the board of directors of the United Refugee Services of Wisconsin (now United Asian Services of Wisconsin) from 1999 to 2005.

# Index

Page numbers in **bold** means that there is a picture on that page.